My Secret Password Book

Password Diary

Activinotes

Activinotes
DAILY JOURNALS, PLANNERS, NOTEBOOKS AND OTHER BLANK BOOKS

Website:_____
Username:_____
Password:_____
Hint:_____
Notes:

_____
_____

Website:_____
Username:_____
Password:_____
Hint:_____
Notes:

_____
_____

Website:_____
Username:_____
Password:_____
Hint:_____
Notes:

_____
_____

Website:_____
Username:_____
Password:_____
Hint:_____
Notes:

_____
_____

Website:_____
Username:_____
Password:_____
Hint:_____
Notes:

_____
_____

Website:_____
Username:_____
Password:_____
Hint:_____
Notes:

_____
_____

Website:_____

Username:_____

Password:_____

Hint:_____

Notes:

_____

_____

_____

Website:_____

Username:_____

Password:_____

Hint:_____

Notes:

_____

_____

_____

Website:_____

Username:_____

Password:_____

Hint:_____

Notes:

_____

_____

_____

Website:_____

Username:_____

Password:_____

Hint:_____

Notes:

_____

_____

_____

Website:_____

Username:_____

Password:_____

Hint:_____

Notes:

_____

_____

_____

Website:_____

Username:_____

Password:_____

Hint:_____

Notes:

_____

_____

_____

Website:_____

Username:_____

Password:_____

Hint:_____

Notes:

_____

_____

Website:_____

Username:_____

Password:_____

Hint:_____

Notes:

_____

_____

Website:_____

Username:_____

Password:_____

Hint:_____

Notes:

_____

_____

Website:_____

Username:_____

Password:_____

Hint:_____

Notes:

_____

_____

Website:_____

Username:_____

Password:_____

Hint:_____

Notes:

_____

_____

Website:_____

Username:_____

Password:_____

Hint:_____

Notes:

_____

_____

Website:_____
Username:_____
Password:_____
Hint:_____
Notes:

_____
_____

Website:_____
Username:_____
Password:_____
Hint:_____
Notes:

_____
_____

Website:_____
Username:_____
Password:_____
Hint:_____
Notes:

_____
_____

Website:_____
Username:_____
Password:_____
Hint:_____
Notes:

_____
_____

Website:_____
Username:_____
Password:_____
Hint:_____
Notes:

_____
_____

Website:_____
Username:_____
Password:_____
Hint:_____
Notes:

_____
_____

Website:_____
Username:_____
Password:_____
Hint:_____
Notes:
_____
_____

Website:_____
Username:_____
Password:_____
Hint:_____
Notes:
_____
_____

Website:_____
Username:_____
Password:_____
Hint:_____
Notes:
_____
_____

Website:_____
Username:_____
Password:_____
Hint:_____
Notes:
_____
_____

Website:_____
Username:_____
Password:_____
Hint:_____
Notes:
_____
_____

Website:_____
Username:_____
Password:_____
Hint:_____
Notes:
_____
_____

Website:_____
Username:_____
Password:_____
Hint:_____
Notes:

_____
_____

Website:_____
Username:_____
Password:_____
Hint:_____
Notes:

_____
_____

Website:_____
Username:_____
Password:_____
Hint:_____
Notes:

_____
_____

Website:_____
Username:_____
Password:_____
Hint:_____
Notes:

_____
_____

Website:_____
Username:_____
Password:_____
Hint:_____
Notes:

_____
_____

Website:_____
Username:_____
Password:_____
Hint:_____
Notes:

_____
_____

Website:_____
Username:_____
Password:_____
Hint:_____
Notes:

_____
_____

Website:_____
Username:_____
Password:_____
Hint:_____
Notes:

_____
_____

Website:_____
Username:_____
Password:_____
Hint:_____
Notes:

_____
_____

Website:_____
Username:_____
Password:_____
Hint:_____
Notes:

_____
_____

Website:_____
Username:_____
Password:_____
Hint:_____
Notes:

_____
_____

Website:_____
Username:_____
Password:_____
Hint:_____
Notes:

_____
_____

Website:_____
Username:_____
Password:_____
Hint:_____
Notes:
_____
_____

Website:_____
Username:_____
Password:_____
Hint:_____
Notes:
_____
_____

Website:_____
Username:_____
Password:_____
Hint:_____
Notes:
_____
_____

Website:_____
Username:_____
Password:_____
Hint:_____
Notes:
_____
_____

Website:_____
Username:_____
Password:_____
Hint:_____
Notes:
_____
_____

Website:_____
Username:_____
Password:_____
Hint:_____
Notes:
_____
_____

Website:_____	
Username:_____	
Password:_____	
Hint:_____	
Notes:	
_____	
_____	

Website:_____	
Username:_____	
Password:_____	
Hint:_____	
Notes:	
_____	
_____	

Website:_____	
Username:_____	
Password:_____	
Hint:_____	
Notes:	
_____	
_____	

Website:_____	
Username:_____	
Password:_____	
Hint:_____	
Notes:	
_____	
_____	

Website:_____	
Username:_____	
Password:_____	
Hint:_____	
Notes:	
_____	
_____	

Website:_____	
Username:_____	
Password:_____	
Hint:_____	
Notes:	
_____	
_____	

Website:
Username:
Password:
Hint:
Notes:

Website:
Username:
Password:
Hint:
Notes:

Website:
Username:
Password:
Hint:
Notes:

Website:
Username:
Password:
Hint:
Notes:

Website:
Username:
Password:
Hint:
Notes:

Website:
Username:
Password:
Hint:
Notes:

Website:_____
Username:_____
Password:_____
Hint:_____
Notes:

_____
_____

Website:_____
Username:_____
Password:_____
Hint:_____
Notes:

_____
_____

Website:_____
Username:_____
Password:_____
Hint:_____
Notes:

_____
_____

Website:_____
Username:_____
Password:_____
Hint:_____
Notes:

_____
_____

Website:_____
Username:_____
Password:_____
Hint:_____
Notes:

_____
_____

Website:_____
Username:_____
Password:_____
Hint:_____
Notes:

_____
_____

Website:_____
Username:_____
Password:_____
Hint:_____
Notes:
_____
_____

Website:_____
Username:_____
Password:_____
Hint:_____
Notes:
_____
_____

Website:_____
Username:_____
Password:_____
Hint:_____
Notes:
_____
_____

Website:_____
Username:_____
Password:_____
Hint:_____
Notes:
_____
_____

Website:_____
Username:_____
Password:_____
Hint:_____
Notes:
_____
_____

Website:_____
Username:_____
Password:_____
Hint:_____
Notes:
_____
_____

Website:_____
Username:_____
Password:_____
Hint:_____
Notes:

_____
_____

Website:_____
Username:_____
Password:_____
Hint:_____
Notes:

_____
_____

Website:_____
Username:_____
Password:_____
Hint:_____
Notes:

_____
_____

Website:_____
Username:_____
Password:_____
Hint:_____
Notes:

_____
_____

Website:_____
Username:_____
Password:_____
Hint:_____
Notes:

_____
_____

Website:_____
Username:_____
Password:_____
Hint:_____
Notes:

_____
_____

Website:_____
Username:_____
Password:_____
Hint:_____
Notes:
_____
_____

Website:_____
Username:_____
Password:_____
Hint:_____
Notes:
_____
_____

Website:_____
Username:_____
Password:_____
Hint:_____
Notes:
_____
_____

Website:_____
Username:_____
Password:_____
Hint:_____
Notes:
_____
_____

Website:_____
Username:_____
Password:_____
Hint:_____
Notes:
_____
_____

Website:_____
Username:_____
Password:_____
Hint:_____
Notes:
_____
_____

Website:_____
Username:_____
Password:_____
Hint:_____
Notes:
_____
_____

Website:_____
Username:_____
Password:_____
Hint:_____
Notes:
_____
_____

Website:_____
Username:_____
Password:_____
Hint:_____
Notes:
_____
_____

Website:_____
Username:_____
Password:_____
Hint:_____
Notes:
_____
_____

Website:_____
Username:_____
Password:_____
Hint:_____
Notes:
_____
_____

Website:_____
Username:_____
Password:_____
Hint:_____
Notes:
_____
_____

Website:_____

Username:_____

Password:_____

Hint:_____

Notes:

_____

_____

Website:_____

Username:_____

Password:_____

Hint:_____

Notes:

_____

_____

Website:_____

Username:_____

Password:_____

Hint:_____

Notes:

_____

_____

Website:_____

Username:_____

Password:_____

Hint:_____

Notes:

_____

_____

Website:_____

Username:_____

Password:_____

Hint:_____

Notes:

_____

_____

Website:_____

Username:_____

Password:_____

Hint:_____

Notes:

_____

_____

Website:_____
Username:_____
Password:_____
Hint:_____
Notes:
_____
_____

Website:_____
Username:_____
Password:_____
Hint:_____
Notes:
_____
_____

Website:_____
Username:_____
Password:_____
Hint:_____
Notes:
_____
_____

Website:_____
Username:_____
Password:_____
Hint:_____
Notes:
_____
_____

Website:_____
Username:_____
Password:_____
Hint:_____
Notes:
_____
_____

Website:_____
Username:_____
Password:_____
Hint:_____
Notes:
_____
_____

Website:_____
Username:_____
Password:_____
Hint:_____
Notes:
_____
_____
_____

Website:_____
Username:_____
Password:_____
Hint:_____
Notes:
_____
_____
_____

Website:_____
Username:_____
Password:_____
Hint:_____
Notes:
_____
_____
_____

Website:_____
Username:_____
Password:_____
Hint:_____
Notes:
_____
_____
_____

Website:_____
Username:_____
Password:_____
Hint:_____
Notes:
_____
_____
_____

Website:_____
Username:_____
Password:_____
Hint:_____
Notes:
_____
_____
_____

Website:_____
Username:_____
Password:_____
Hint:_____
Notes:

_____
_____

Website:_____
Username:_____
Password:_____
Hint:_____
Notes:

_____
_____

Website:_____
Username:_____
Password:_____
Hint:_____
Notes:

_____
_____

Website:_____
Username:_____
Password:_____
Hint:_____
Notes:

_____
_____

Website:_____
Username:_____
Password:_____
Hint:_____
Notes:

_____
_____

Website:_____
Username:_____
Password:_____
Hint:_____
Notes:

_____
_____

Website:_____
Username:_____
Password:_____
Hint:_____
Notes:
_____
_____

Website:_____
Username:_____
Password:_____
Hint:_____
Notes:
_____
_____

Website:_____
Username:_____
Password:_____
Hint:_____
Notes:
_____
_____

Website:_____
Username:_____
Password:_____
Hint:_____
Notes:
_____
_____

Website:_____
Username:_____
Password:_____
Hint:_____
Notes:
_____
_____

Website:_____
Username:_____
Password:_____
Hint:_____
Notes:
_____
_____

Website:_____
Username:_____
Password:_____
Hint:_____
Notes:

_____
_____

Website:_____
Username:_____
Password:_____
Hint:_____
Notes:

_____
_____

Website:_____
Username:_____
Password:_____
Hint:_____
Notes:

_____
_____

Website:_____
Username:_____
Password:_____
Hint:_____
Notes:

_____
_____

Website:_____
Username:_____
Password:_____
Hint:_____
Notes:

_____
_____

Website:_____
Username:_____
Password:_____
Hint:_____
Notes:

_____
_____

Website:_____
Username:_____
Password:_____
Hint:_____
Notes:

_____
_____

Website:_____
Username:_____
Password:_____
Hint:_____
Notes:

_____
_____

Website:_____
Username:_____
Password:_____
Hint:_____
Notes:

_____
_____

Website:_____
Username:_____
Password:_____
Hint:_____
Notes:

_____
_____

Website:_____
Username:_____
Password:_____
Hint:_____
Notes:

_____
_____

Website:_____
Username:_____
Password:_____
Hint:_____
Notes:

_____
_____

Website:_____

Username:_____

Password:_____

Hint:_____

Notes:

_____

_____

Website:_____

Username:_____

Password:_____

Hint:_____

Notes:

_____

_____

Website:_____

Username:_____

Password:_____

Hint:_____

Notes:

_____

_____

Website:_____

Username:_____

Password:_____

Hint:_____

Notes:

_____

_____

Website:_____

Username:_____

Password:_____

Hint:_____

Notes:

_____

_____

Website:_____

Username:_____

Password:_____

Hint:_____

Notes:

_____

_____

Website:_____
Username:_____
Password:_____
Hint:_____
Notes:
_____
_____
_____

Website:_____
Username:_____
Password:_____
Hint:_____
Notes:
_____
_____
_____

Website:_____
Username:_____
Password:_____
Hint:_____
Notes:
_____
_____
_____

Website:_____
Username:_____
Password:_____
Hint:_____
Notes:
_____
_____
_____

Website:_____
Username:_____
Password:_____
Hint:_____
Notes:
_____
_____
_____

Website:_____
Username:_____
Password:_____
Hint:_____
Notes:
_____
_____
_____

Website:_____
Username:_____
Password:_____
Hint:_____
Notes:
_____
_____

Website:_____
Username:_____
Password:_____
Hint:_____
Notes:
_____
_____

Website:_____
Username:_____
Password:_____
Hint:_____
Notes:
_____
_____

Website:_____
Username:_____
Password:_____
Hint:_____
Notes:
_____
_____

Website:_____
Username:_____
Password:_____
Hint:_____
Notes:
_____
_____

Website:_____
Username:_____
Password:_____
Hint:_____
Notes:
_____
_____

Website:_____
Username:_____
Password:_____
Hint:_____
Notes:
_____
_____

Website:_____
Username:_____
Password:_____
Hint:_____
Notes:
_____
_____

Website:_____
Username:_____
Password:_____
Hint:_____
Notes:
_____
_____

Website:_____
Username:_____
Password:_____
Hint:_____
Notes:
_____
_____

Website:_____
Username:_____
Password:_____
Hint:_____
Notes:
_____
_____

Website:_____
Username:_____
Password:_____
Hint:_____
Notes:
_____
_____

Website:_____
Username:_____
Password:_____
Hint:_____
Notes:
_____
_____

Website:_____
Username:_____
Password:_____
Hint:_____
Notes:
_____
_____

Website:_____
Username:_____
Password:_____
Hint:_____
Notes:
_____
_____

Website:_____
Username:_____
Password:_____
Hint:_____
Notes:
_____
_____

Website:_____
Username:_____
Password:_____
Hint:_____
Notes:
_____
_____

Website:_____
Username:_____
Password:_____
Hint:_____
Notes:
_____
_____

Website:_____

Username:_____

Password:_____

Hint:_____

Notes:

_____

_____

Website:_____

Username:_____

Password:_____

Hint:_____

Notes:

_____

_____

Website:_____

Username:_____

Password:_____

Hint:_____

Notes:

_____

_____

Website:_____

Username:_____

Password:_____

Hint:_____

Notes:

_____

_____

Website:_____

Username:_____

Password:_____

Hint:_____

Notes:

_____

_____

Website:_____

Username:_____

Password:_____

Hint:_____

Notes:

_____

_____

Website:_____
Username:_____
Password:_____
Hint:_____
Notes:
_____
_____

Website:_____
Username:_____
Password:_____
Hint:_____
Notes:
_____
_____

Website:_____
Username:_____
Password:_____
Hint:_____
Notes:
_____
_____

Website:_____
Username:_____
Password:_____
Hint:_____
Notes:
_____
_____

Website:_____
Username:_____
Password:_____
Hint:_____
Notes:
_____
_____

Website:_____
Username:_____
Password:_____
Hint:_____
Notes:
_____
_____

Website:_____
Username:_____
Password:_____
Hint:_____
Notes:
_____
_____

Website:_____
Username:_____
Password:_____
Hint:_____
Notes:
_____
_____

Website:_____
Username:_____
Password:_____
Hint:_____
Notes:
_____
_____

Website:_____
Username:_____
Password:_____
Hint:_____
Notes:
_____
_____

Website:_____
Username:_____
Password:_____
Hint:_____
Notes:
_____
_____

Website:_____
Username:_____
Password:_____
Hint:_____
Notes:
_____
_____

Website:_____

Username:_____

Password:_____

Hint:_____

Notes:

_____

_____

Website:_____

Username:_____

Password:_____

Hint:_____

Notes:

_____

_____

Website:_____

Username:_____

Password:_____

Hint:_____

Notes:

_____

_____

Website:_____

Username:_____

Password:_____

Hint:_____

Notes:

_____

_____

Website:_____

Username:_____

Password:_____

Hint:_____

Notes:

_____

_____

Website:_____

Username:_____

Password:_____

Hint:_____

Notes:

_____

_____

Website:_____
Username:_____
Password:_____
Hint:_____
Notes:
_____
_____

Website:_____
Username:_____
Password:_____
Hint:_____
Notes:
_____
_____

Website:_____
Username:_____
Password:_____
Hint:_____
Notes:
_____
_____

Website:_____
Username:_____
Password:_____
Hint:_____
Notes:
_____
_____

Website:_____
Username:_____
Password:_____
Hint:_____
Notes:
_____
_____

Website:_____
Username:_____
Password:_____
Hint:_____
Notes:
_____
_____

Website:_____
Username:_____
Password:_____
Hint:_____
Notes:

_____
_____

Website:_____
Username:_____
Password:_____
Hint:_____
Notes:

_____
_____

Website:_____
Username:_____
Password:_____
Hint:_____
Notes:

_____
_____

Website:_____
Username:_____
Password:_____
Hint:_____
Notes:

_____
_____

Website:_____
Username:_____
Password:_____
Hint:_____
Notes:

_____
_____

Website:_____
Username:_____
Password:_____
Hint:_____
Notes:

_____
_____

Website:_____

Username:_____

Password:_____

Hint:_____

Notes:

_____

_____

Website:_____

Username:_____

Password:_____

Hint:_____

Notes:

_____

_____

Website:_____

Username:_____

Password:_____

Hint:_____

Notes:

_____

_____

Website:_____

Username:_____

Password:_____

Hint:_____

Notes:

_____

_____

Website:_____

Username:_____

Password:_____

Hint:_____

Notes:

_____

_____

Website:_____

Username:_____

Password:_____

Hint:_____

Notes:

_____

_____

Website:_____
Username:_____
Password:_____
Hint:_____
Notes:
_____
_____

Website:_____
Username:_____
Password:_____
Hint:_____
Notes:
_____
_____

Website:_____
Username:_____
Password:_____
Hint:_____
Notes:
_____
_____

Website:_____
Username:_____
Password:_____
Hint:_____
Notes:
_____
_____

Website:_____
Username:_____
Password:_____
Hint:_____
Notes:
_____
_____

Website:_____
Username:_____
Password:_____
Hint:_____
Notes:
_____
_____

Website:_____
Username:_____
Password:_____
Hint:_____
Notes:
_____
_____

Website:_____
Username:_____
Password:_____
Hint:_____
Notes:
_____
_____

Website:_____
Username:_____
Password:_____
Hint:_____
Notes:
_____
_____

Website:_____
Username:_____
Password:_____
Hint:_____
Notes:
_____
_____

Website:_____
Username:_____
Password:_____
Hint:_____
Notes:
_____
_____

Website:_____
Username:_____
Password:_____
Hint:_____
Notes:
_____
_____

Website:_____

Username:_____

Password:_____

Hint:_____

Notes:

_____

_____

Website:_____

Username:_____

Password:_____

Hint:_____

Notes:

_____

_____

Website:_____

Username:_____

Password:_____

Hint:_____

Notes:

_____

_____

Website:_____

Username:_____

Password:_____

Hint:_____

Notes:

_____

_____

Website:_____

Username:_____

Password:_____

Hint:_____

Notes:

_____

_____

Website:_____

Username:_____

Password:_____

Hint:_____

Notes:

_____

_____

Website:_____
Username:_____
Password:_____
Hint:_____
Notes:
_____
_____

Website:_____
Username:_____
Password:_____
Hint:_____
Notes:
_____
_____

Website:_____
Username:_____
Password:_____
Hint:_____
Notes:
_____
_____

Website:_____
Username:_____
Password:_____
Hint:_____
Notes:
_____
_____

Website:_____
Username:_____
Password:_____
Hint:_____
Notes:
_____
_____

Website:_____
Username:_____
Password:_____
Hint:_____
Notes:
_____
_____

Website:_____
Username:_____
Password:_____
Hint:_____
Notes:
_____
_____

Website:_____
Username:_____
Password:_____
Hint:_____
Notes:
_____
_____

Website:_____
Username:_____
Password:_____
Hint:_____
Notes:
_____
_____

Website:_____
Username:_____
Password:_____
Hint:_____
Notes:
_____
_____

Website:_____
Username:_____
Password:_____
Hint:_____
Notes:
_____
_____

Website:_____
Username:_____
Password:_____
Hint:_____
Notes:
_____
_____

Website:_____
Username:_____
Password:_____
Hint:_____
Notes:

_____
_____

Website:_____
Username:_____
Password:_____
Hint:_____
Notes:

_____
_____

Website:_____
Username:_____
Password:_____
Hint:_____
Notes:

_____
_____

Website:_____
Username:_____
Password:_____
Hint:_____
Notes:

_____
_____

Website:_____
Username:_____
Password:_____
Hint:_____
Notes:

_____
_____

Website:_____
Username:_____
Password:_____
Hint:_____
Notes:

_____
_____

Website:_____
Username:_____
Password:_____
Hint:_____
Notes:

_____
_____

Website:_____
Username:_____
Password:_____
Hint:_____
Notes:

_____
_____

Website:_____
Username:_____
Password:_____
Hint:_____
Notes:

_____
_____

Website:_____
Username:_____
Password:_____
Hint:_____
Notes:

_____
_____

Website:_____
Username:_____
Password:_____
Hint:_____
Notes:

_____
_____

Website:_____
Username:_____
Password:_____
Hint:_____
Notes:

_____
_____

Website:_____
Username:_____
Password:_____
Hint:_____
Notes:
_____
_____

Website:_____
Username:_____
Password:_____
Hint:_____
Notes:
_____
_____

Website:_____
Username:_____
Password:_____
Hint:_____
Notes:
_____
_____

Website:_____
Username:_____
Password:_____
Hint:_____
Notes:
_____
_____

Website:_____
Username:_____
Password:_____
Hint:_____
Notes:
_____
_____

Website:_____
Username:_____
Password:_____
Hint:_____
Notes:
_____
_____

Website:_____
Username:_____
Password:_____
Hint:_____
Notes:

_____
_____

Website:_____
Username:_____
Password:_____
Hint:_____
Notes:

_____
_____

Website:_____
Username:_____
Password:_____
Hint:_____
Notes:

_____
_____

Website:_____
Username:_____
Password:_____
Hint:_____
Notes:

_____
_____

Website:_____
Username:_____
Password:_____
Hint:_____
Notes:

_____
_____

Website:_____
Username:_____
Password:_____
Hint:_____
Notes:

_____
_____

Website:_____
Username:_____
Password:_____
Hint:_____
Notes:

_____
_____

Website:_____
Username:_____
Password:_____
Hint:_____
Notes:

_____
_____

Website:_____
Username:_____
Password:_____
Hint:_____
Notes:

_____
_____

Website:_____
Username:_____
Password:_____
Hint:_____
Notes:

_____
_____

Website:_____
Username:_____
Password:_____
Hint:_____
Notes:

_____
_____

Website:_____
Username:_____
Password:_____
Hint:_____
Notes:

_____
_____

Website:_____
Username:_____
Password:_____
Hint:_____
Notes:

_____
_____

Website:_____
Username:_____
Password:_____
Hint:_____
Notes:

_____
_____

Website:_____
Username:_____
Password:_____
Hint:_____
Notes:

_____
_____

Website:_____
Username:_____
Password:_____
Hint:_____
Notes:

_____
_____

Website:_____
Username:_____
Password:_____
Hint:_____
Notes:

_____
_____

Website:_____
Username:_____
Password:_____
Hint:_____
Notes:

_____
_____

Website:_____
Username:_____
Password:_____
Hint:_____
Notes:
_____
_____
_____

Website:_____
Username:_____
Password:_____
Hint:_____
Notes:
_____
_____
_____

Website:_____
Username:_____
Password:_____
Hint:_____
Notes:
_____
_____
_____

Website:_____
Username:_____
Password:_____
Hint:_____
Notes:
_____
_____
_____

Website:_____
Username:_____
Password:_____
Hint:_____
Notes:
_____
_____
_____

Website:_____
Username:_____
Password:_____
Hint:_____
Notes:
_____
_____

Website:_____
Username:_____
Password:_____
Hint:_____
Notes:

_____
_____

Website:_____
Username:_____
Password:_____
Hint:_____
Notes:

_____
_____

Website:_____
Username:_____
Password:_____
Hint:_____
Notes:

_____
_____

Website:_____
Username:_____
Password:_____
Hint:_____
Notes:

_____
_____

Website:_____
Username:_____
Password:_____
Hint:_____
Notes:

_____
_____

Website:_____
Username:_____
Password:_____
Hint:_____
Notes:

_____
_____

Website:_____
Username:_____
Password:_____
Hint:_____
Notes:
_____
_____

Website:_____
Username:_____
Password:_____
Hint:_____
Notes:
_____
_____

Website:_____
Username:_____
Password:_____
Hint:_____
Notes:
_____
_____

Website:_____
Username:_____
Password:_____
Hint:_____
Notes:
_____
_____

Website:_____
Username:_____
Password:_____
Hint:_____
Notes:
_____
_____

Website:_____
Username:_____
Password:_____
Hint:_____
Notes:
_____
_____

Website:_____
Username:_____
Password:_____
Hint:_____
Notes:

_____
_____

Website:_____
Username:_____
Password:_____
Hint:_____
Notes:

_____
_____

Website:_____
Username:_____
Password:_____
Hint:_____
Notes:

_____
_____

Website:_____
Username:_____
Password:_____
Hint:_____
Notes:

_____
_____

Website:_____
Username:_____
Password:_____
Hint:_____
Notes:

_____
_____

Website:_____
Username:_____
Password:_____
Hint:_____
Notes:

_____
_____

Website:_____
Username:_____
Password:_____
Hint:_____
Notes:
_____
_____
_____

Website:_____
Username:_____
Password:_____
Hint:_____
Notes:
_____
_____
_____

Website:_____
Username:_____
Password:_____
Hint:_____
Notes:
_____
_____
_____

Website:_____
Username:_____
Password:_____
Hint:_____
Notes:
_____
_____
_____

Website:_____
Username:_____
Password:_____
Hint:_____
Notes:
_____
_____
_____

Website:_____
Username:_____
Password:_____
Hint:_____
Notes:
_____
_____
_____

Website:_____
Username:_____
Password:_____
Hint:_____
Notes:

_____
_____

Website:_____
Username:_____
Password:_____
Hint:_____
Notes:

_____
_____

Website:_____
Username:_____
Password:_____
Hint:_____
Notes:

_____
_____

Website:_____
Username:_____
Password:_____
Hint:_____
Notes:

_____
_____

Website:_____
Username:_____
Password:_____
Hint:_____
Notes:

_____
_____

Website:_____
Username:_____
Password:_____
Hint:_____
Notes:

_____
_____

Website:_____

Username:_____

Password:_____

Hint:_____

Notes:
_____
_____

Website:_____

Username:_____

Password:_____

Hint:_____

Notes:
_____
_____

Website:_____

Username:_____

Password:_____

Hint:_____

Notes:
_____
_____

Website:_____

Username:_____

Password:_____

Hint:_____

Notes:
_____
_____

Website:_____

Username:_____

Password:_____

Hint:_____

Notes:
_____
_____

Website:_____

Username:_____

Password:_____

Hint:_____

Notes:
_____
_____

Website:_____
Username:_____
Password:_____
Hint:_____
Notes:

_____
_____

Website:_____
Username:_____
Password:_____
Hint:_____
Notes:

_____
_____

Website:_____
Username:_____
Password:_____
Hint:_____
Notes:

_____
_____

Website:_____
Username:_____
Password:_____
Hint:_____
Notes:

_____
_____

Website:_____
Username:_____
Password:_____
Hint:_____
Notes:

_____
_____

Website:_____
Username:_____
Password:_____
Hint:_____
Notes:

_____
_____

Website:_____
Username:_____
Password:_____
Hint:_____
Notes:
_____
_____

Website:_____
Username:_____
Password:_____
Hint:_____
Notes:
_____
_____

Website:_____
Username:_____
Password:_____
Hint:_____
Notes:
_____
_____

Website:_____
Username:_____
Password:_____
Hint:_____
Notes:
_____
_____

Website:_____
Username:_____
Password:_____
Hint:_____
Notes:
_____
_____

Website:_____
Username:_____
Password:_____
Hint:_____
Notes:
_____
_____

Website:_____
Username:_____
Password:_____
Hint:_____
Notes:
_____
_____

Website:_____
Username:_____
Password:_____
Hint:_____
Notes:
_____
_____

Website:_____
Username:_____
Password:_____
Hint:_____
Notes:
_____
_____

Website:_____
Username:_____
Password:_____
Hint:_____
Notes:
_____
_____

Website:_____
Username:_____
Password:_____
Hint:_____
Notes:
_____
_____

Website:_____
Username:_____
Password:_____
Hint:_____
Notes:
_____
_____

Website:_____
Username:_____
Password:_____
Hint:_____
Notes:
_____
_____

Website:_____
Username:_____
Password:_____
Hint:_____
Notes:
_____
_____

Website:_____
Username:_____
Password:_____
Hint:_____
Notes:
_____
_____

Website:_____
Username:_____
Password:_____
Hint:_____
Notes:
_____
_____

Website:_____
Username:_____
Password:_____
Hint:_____
Notes:
_____
_____

Website:_____
Username:_____
Password:_____
Hint:_____
Notes:
_____
_____

Website:_____
Username:_____
Password:_____
Hint:_____
Notes:

_____
_____

Website:_____
Username:_____
Password:_____
Hint:_____
Notes:

_____
_____

Website:_____
Username:_____
Password:_____
Hint:_____
Notes:

_____
_____

Website:_____
Username:_____
Password:_____
Hint:_____
Notes:

_____
_____

Website:_____
Username:_____
Password:_____
Hint:_____
Notes:

_____
_____

Website:_____
Username:_____
Password:_____
Hint:_____
Notes:

_____
_____

Website:_____
Username:_____
Password:_____
Hint:_____
Notes:
_____
_____

Website:_____
Username:_____
Password:_____
Hint:_____
Notes:
_____
_____

Website:_____
Username:_____
Password:_____
Hint:_____
Notes:
_____
_____

Website:_____
Username:_____
Password:_____
Hint:_____
Notes:
_____
_____

Website:_____
Username:_____
Password:_____
Hint:_____
Notes:
_____
_____

Website:_____
Username:_____
Password:_____
Hint:_____
Notes:
_____
_____

Website:_____
Username:_____
Password:_____
Hint:_____
Notes:
_____
_____

Website:_____
Username:_____
Password:_____
Hint:_____
Notes:
_____
_____

Website:_____
Username:_____
Password:_____
Hint:_____
Notes:
_____
_____

Website:_____
Username:_____
Password:_____
Hint:_____
Notes:
_____
_____

Website:_____
Username:_____
Password:_____
Hint:_____
Notes:
_____
_____

Website:_____
Username:_____
Password:_____
Hint:_____
Notes:
_____
_____

Website:_____

Username:_____

Password:_____

Hint:_____

Notes:

_____

_____

Website:_____

Username:_____

Password:_____

Hint:_____

Notes:

_____

_____

Website:_____

Username:_____

Password:_____

Hint:_____

Notes:

_____

_____

Website:_____

Username:_____

Password:_____

Hint:_____

Notes:

_____

_____

Website:_____

Username:_____

Password:_____

Hint:_____

Notes:

_____

_____

Website:_____

Username:_____

Password:_____

Hint:_____

Notes:

_____

_____

Website:_____
Username:_____
Password:_____
Hint:_____
Notes:
_____
_____

Website:_____
Username:_____
Password:_____
Hint:_____
Notes:
_____
_____

Website:_____
Username:_____
Password:_____
Hint:_____
Notes:
_____
_____

Website:_____
Username:_____
Password:_____
Hint:_____
Notes:
_____
_____

Website:_____
Username:_____
Password:_____
Hint:_____
Notes:
_____
_____

Website:_____
Username:_____
Password:_____
Hint:_____
Notes:
_____
_____

Website:_____
Username:_____
Password:_____
Hint:_____
Notes:
_____
_____

Website:_____
Username:_____
Password:_____
Hint:_____
Notes:
_____
_____

Website:_____
Username:_____
Password:_____
Hint:_____
Notes:
_____
_____

Website:_____
Username:_____
Password:_____
Hint:_____
Notes:
_____
_____

Website:_____
Username:_____
Password:_____
Hint:_____
Notes:
_____
_____

Website:_____
Username:_____
Password:_____
Hint:_____
Notes:
_____
_____

Website:_____

Username:_____

Password:_____

Hint:_____

Notes:

_____

_____

Website:_____

Username:_____

Password:_____

Hint:_____

Notes:

_____

_____

Website:_____

Username:_____

Password:_____

Hint:_____

Notes:

_____

_____

Website:_____

Username:_____

Password:_____

Hint:_____

Notes:

_____

_____

Website:_____

Username:_____

Password:_____

Hint:_____

Notes:

_____

_____

Website:_____

Username:_____

Password:_____

Hint:_____

Notes:

_____

_____

Website:_____

Username:_____

Password:_____

Hint:_____

Notes:

_____

_____

Website:_____

Username:_____

Password:_____

Hint:_____

Notes:

_____

_____

Website:_____

Username:_____

Password:_____

Hint:_____

Notes:

_____

_____

Website:_____

Username:_____

Password:_____

Hint:_____

Notes:

_____

_____

Website:_____

Username:_____

Password:_____

Hint:_____

Notes:

_____

_____

Website:_____

Username:_____

Password:_____

Hint:_____

Notes:

_____

_____

Website:_____
Username:_____
Password:_____
Hint:_____
Notes:
_____
_____

Website:_____
Username:_____
Password:_____
Hint:_____
Notes:
_____
_____

Website:_____
Username:_____
Password:_____
Hint:_____
Notes:
_____
_____

Website:_____
Username:_____
Password:_____
Hint:_____
Notes:
_____
_____

Website:_____
Username:_____
Password:_____
Hint:_____
Notes:
_____
_____

Website:_____
Username:_____
Password:_____
Hint:_____
Notes:
_____
_____

Website:_____
Username:_____
Password:_____
Hint:_____
Notes:

_____
_____

Website:_____
Username:_____
Password:_____
Hint:_____
Notes:

_____
_____

Website:_____
Username:_____
Password:_____
Hint:_____
Notes:

_____
_____

Website:_____
Username:_____
Password:_____
Hint:_____
Notes:

_____
_____

Website:_____
Username:_____
Password:_____
Hint:_____
Notes:

_____
_____

Website:_____
Username:_____
Password:_____
Hint:_____
Notes:

_____
_____

Website:_____
Username:_____
Password:_____
Hint:_____
Notes:

_____
_____

Website:_____
Username:_____
Password:_____
Hint:_____
Notes:

_____
_____

Website:_____
Username:_____
Password:_____
Hint:_____
Notes:

_____
_____

Website:_____
Username:_____
Password:_____
Hint:_____
Notes:

_____
_____

Website:_____
Username:_____
Password:_____
Hint:_____
Notes:

_____
_____

Website:_____
Username:_____
Password:_____
Hint:_____
Notes:

_____
_____

Website:_____
Username:_____
Password:_____
Hint:_____
Notes:
_____
_____

Website:_____
Username:_____
Password:_____
Hint:_____
Notes:
_____
_____

Website:_____
Username:_____
Password:_____
Hint:_____
Notes:
_____
_____

Website:_____
Username:_____
Password:_____
Hint:_____
Notes:
_____
_____

Website:_____
Username:_____
Password:_____
Hint:_____
Notes:
_____
_____

Website:_____
Username:_____
Password:_____
Hint:_____
Notes:
_____
_____

Website:_____
Username:_____
Password:_____
Hint:_____
Notes:
_____
_____

Website:_____
Username:_____
Password:_____
Hint:_____
Notes:
_____
_____

Website:_____
Username:_____
Password:_____
Hint:_____
Notes:
_____
_____

Website:_____
Username:_____
Password:_____
Hint:_____
Notes:
_____
_____

Website:_____
Username:_____
Password:_____
Hint:_____
Notes:
_____
_____

Website:_____
Username:_____
Password:_____
Hint:_____
Notes:
_____
_____

Website:_____
Username:_____
Password:_____
Hint:_____
Notes:
_____
_____

Website:_____
Username:_____
Password:_____
Hint:_____
Notes:
_____
_____

Website:_____
Username:_____
Password:_____
Hint:_____
Notes:
_____
_____

Website:_____
Username:_____
Password:_____
Hint:_____
Notes:
_____
_____

Website:_____
Username:_____
Password:_____
Hint:_____
Notes:
_____
_____

Website:_____
Username:_____
Password:_____
Hint:_____
Notes:
_____
_____

Website:_____
Username:_____
Password:_____
Hint:_____
Notes:

_____
_____

Website:_____
Username:_____
Password:_____
Hint:_____
Notes:

_____
_____

Website:_____
Username:_____
Password:_____
Hint:_____
Notes:

_____
_____

Website:_____
Username:_____
Password:_____
Hint:_____
Notes:

_____
_____

Website:_____
Username:_____
Password:_____
Hint:_____
Notes:

_____
_____

Website:_____
Username:_____
Password:_____
Hint:_____
Notes:

_____
_____

Website:_____

Username:_____

Password:_____

Hint:_____

Notes:

_____

_____

Website:_____

Username:_____

Password:_____

Hint:_____

Notes:

_____

_____

Website:_____

Username:_____

Password:_____

Hint:_____

Notes:

_____

_____

Website:_____

Username:_____

Password:_____

Hint:_____

Notes:

_____

_____

Website:_____

Username:_____

Password:_____

Hint:_____

Notes:

_____

_____

Website:_____

Username:_____

Password:_____

Hint:_____

Notes:

_____

_____

Website:_____
Username:_____
Password:_____
Hint:_____
Notes:

_____
_____

Website:_____
Username:_____
Password:_____
Hint:_____
Notes:

_____
_____

Website:_____
Username:_____
Password:_____
Hint:_____
Notes:

_____
_____

Website:_____
Username:_____
Password:_____
Hint:_____
Notes:

_____
_____

Website:_____
Username:_____
Password:_____
Hint:_____
Notes:

_____
_____

Website:_____
Username:_____
Password:_____
Hint:_____
Notes:

_____
_____

Website:_____

Username:_____

Password:_____

Hint:_____

Notes:

_____

_____

Website:_____

Username:_____

Password:_____

Hint:_____

Notes:

_____

_____

Website:_____

Username:_____

Password:_____

Hint:_____

Notes:

_____

_____

Website:_____

Username:_____

Password:_____

Hint:_____

Notes:

_____

_____

Website:_____

Username:_____

Password:_____

Hint:_____

Notes:

_____

_____

Website:_____

Username:_____

Password:_____

Hint:_____

Notes:

_____

_____

Website:_____
Username:_____
Password:_____
Hint:_____
Notes:

_____
_____

Website:_____
Username:_____
Password:_____
Hint:_____
Notes:

_____
_____

Website:_____
Username:_____
Password:_____
Hint:_____
Notes:

_____
_____

Website:_____
Username:_____
Password:_____
Hint:_____
Notes:

_____
_____

Website:_____
Username:_____
Password:_____
Hint:_____
Notes:

_____
_____

Website:_____
Username:_____
Password:_____
Hint:_____
Notes:

_____
_____

Website:_____
Username:_____
Password:_____
Hint:_____
Notes:
_____
_____

Website:_____
Username:_____
Password:_____
Hint:_____
Notes:
_____
_____

Website:_____
Username:_____
Password:_____
Hint:_____
Notes:
_____
_____

Website:_____
Username:_____
Password:_____
Hint:_____
Notes:
_____
_____

Website:_____
Username:_____
Password:_____
Hint:_____
Notes:
_____
_____

Website:_____
Username:_____
Password:_____
Hint:_____
Notes:
_____
_____

Website:_____
Username:_____
Password:_____
Hint:_____
Notes:

_____
_____

Website:_____
Username:_____
Password:_____
Hint:_____
Notes:

_____
_____

Website:_____
Username:_____
Password:_____
Hint:_____
Notes:

_____
_____

Website:_____
Username:_____
Password:_____
Hint:_____
Notes:

_____
_____

Website:_____
Username:_____
Password:_____
Hint:_____
Notes:

_____
_____

Website:_____
Username:_____
Password:_____
Hint:_____
Notes:

_____
_____

Website:_____
Username:_____
Password:_____
Hint:_____
Notes:
_____
_____

Website:_____
Username:_____
Password:_____
Hint:_____
Notes:
_____
_____

Website:_____
Username:_____
Password:_____
Hint:_____
Notes:
_____
_____

Website:_____
Username:_____
Password:_____
Hint:_____
Notes:
_____
_____

Website:_____
Username:_____
Password:_____
Hint:_____
Notes:
_____
_____

Website:_____
Username:_____
Password:_____
Hint:_____
Notes:
_____
_____

Website:_____
Username:_____
Password:_____
Hint:_____
Notes:
_____
_____

Website:_____
Username:_____
Password:_____
Hint:_____
Notes:
_____
_____

Website:_____
Username:_____
Password:_____
Hint:_____
Notes:
_____
_____

Website:_____
Username:_____
Password:_____
Hint:_____
Notes:
_____
_____

Website:_____
Username:_____
Password:_____
Hint:_____
Notes:
_____
_____

Website:_____
Username:_____
Password:_____
Hint:_____
Notes:
_____
_____

Website:_____

Username:_____

Password:_____

Hint:_____

Notes:_____

_____

_____

Website:_____

Username:_____

Password:_____

Hint:_____

Notes:_____

_____

_____

Website:_____

Username:_____

Password:_____

Hint:_____

Notes:_____

_____

_____

Website:_____

Username:_____

Password:_____

Hint:_____

Notes:_____

_____

_____

Website:_____

Username:_____

Password:_____

Hint:_____

Notes:_____

_____

_____

Website:_____

Username:_____

Password:_____

Hint:_____

Notes:_____

_____

_____

Website:_____
Username:_____
Password:_____
Hint:_____
Notes:

_____
_____

Website:_____
Username:_____
Password:_____
Hint:_____
Notes:

_____
_____

Website:_____
Username:_____
Password:_____
Hint:_____
Notes:

_____
_____

Website:_____
Username:_____
Password:_____
Hint:_____
Notes:

_____
_____

Website:_____
Username:_____
Password:_____
Hint:_____
Notes:

_____
_____

Website:_____
Username:_____
Password:_____
Hint:_____
Notes:

_____
_____

Website:_____
Username:_____
Password:_____
Hint:_____
Notes:
_____
_____
_____

Website:_____
Username:_____
Password:_____
Hint:_____
Notes:
_____
_____
_____

Website:_____
Username:_____
Password:_____
Hint:_____
Notes:
_____
_____
_____

Website:_____
Username:_____
Password:_____
Hint:_____
Notes:
_____
_____
_____

Website:_____
Username:_____
Password:_____
Hint:_____
Notes:
_____
_____
_____

Website:_____
Username:_____
Password:_____
Hint:_____
Notes:
_____
_____
_____

Website:_____
Username:_____
Password:_____
Hint:_____
Notes:

_____
_____

Website:_____
Username:_____
Password:_____
Hint:_____
Notes:

_____
_____

Website:_____
Username:_____
Password:_____
Hint:_____
Notes:

_____
_____

Website:_____
Username:_____
Password:_____
Hint:_____
Notes:

_____
_____

Website:_____
Username:_____
Password:_____
Hint:_____
Notes:

_____
_____

Website:_____
Username:_____
Password:_____
Hint:_____
Notes:

_____
_____

Website:_____
Username:_____
Password:_____
Hint:_____
Notes:

_____
_____

Website:_____
Username:_____
Password:_____
Hint:_____
Notes:

_____
_____

Website:_____
Username:_____
Password:_____
Hint:_____
Notes:

_____
_____

Website:_____
Username:_____
Password:_____
Hint:_____
Notes:

_____
_____

Website:_____
Username:_____
Password:_____
Hint:_____
Notes:

_____
_____

Website:_____
Username:_____
Password:_____
Hint:_____
Notes:

_____
_____

Website:_____
Username:_____
Password:_____
Hint:_____
Notes:
_____
_____
_____

Website:_____
Username:_____
Password:_____
Hint:_____
Notes:
_____
_____
_____

Website:_____
Username:_____
Password:_____
Hint:_____
Notes:
_____
_____
_____

Website:_____
Username:_____
Password:_____
Hint:_____
Notes:
_____
_____
_____

Website:_____
Username:_____
Password:_____
Hint:_____
Notes:
_____
_____
_____

Website:_____
Username:_____
Password:_____
Hint:_____
Notes:
_____
_____
_____

Website:_____
Username:_____
Password:_____
Hint:_____
Notes:
_____
_____

Website:_____
Username:_____
Password:_____
Hint:_____
Notes:
_____
_____

Website:_____
Username:_____
Password:_____
Hint:_____
Notes:
_____
_____

Website:_____
Username:_____
Password:_____
Hint:_____
Notes:
_____
_____

Website:_____
Username:_____
Password:_____
Hint:_____
Notes:
_____
_____

Website:_____
Username:_____
Password:_____
Hint:_____
Notes:
_____
_____

Website:_____
Username:_____
Password:_____
Hint:_____
Notes:

_____
_____

Website:_____
Username:_____
Password:_____
Hint:_____
Notes:

_____
_____

Website:_____
Username:_____
Password:_____
Hint:_____
Notes:

_____
_____

Website:_____
Username:_____
Password:_____
Hint:_____
Notes:

_____
_____

Website:_____
Username:_____
Password:_____
Hint:_____
Notes:

_____
_____

Website:_____
Username:_____
Password:_____
Hint:_____
Notes:

_____
_____

Website:_____
Username:_____
Password:_____
Hint:_____
Notes:
_____
_____

Website:_____
Username:_____
Password:_____
Hint:_____
Notes:
_____
_____

Website:_____
Username:_____
Password:_____
Hint:_____
Notes:
_____
_____

Website:_____
Username:_____
Password:_____
Hint:_____
Notes:
_____
_____

Website:_____
Username:_____
Password:_____
Hint:_____
Notes:
_____
_____

Website:_____
Username:_____
Password:_____
Hint:_____
Notes:
_____
_____

Website:_____

Username:_____

Password:_____

Hint:_____

Notes:

_____

_____

Website:_____

Username:_____

Password:_____

Hint:_____

Notes:

_____

_____

Website:_____

Username:_____

Password:_____

Hint:_____

Notes:

_____

_____

Website:_____

Username:_____

Password:_____

Hint:_____

Notes:

_____

_____

Website:_____

Username:_____

Password:_____

Hint:_____

Notes:

_____

_____

Website:_____

Username:_____

Password:_____

Hint:_____

Notes:

_____

_____

Website:_____ Username:_____ Password:_____ Hint:_____ Notes: _____ _____
Website:_____ Username:_____ Password:_____ Hint:_____ Notes: _____ _____
Website:_____ Username:_____ Password:_____ Hint:_____ Notes: _____ _____
Website:_____ Username:_____ Password:_____ Hint:_____ Notes: _____ _____
Website:_____ Username:_____ Password:_____ Hint:_____ Notes: _____ _____
Website:_____ Username:_____ Password:_____ Hint:_____ Notes: _____ _____

Website:_____
Username:_____
Password:_____
Hint:_____
Notes:
_____
_____

Website:_____
Username:_____
Password:_____
Hint:_____
Notes:
_____
_____

Website:_____
Username:_____
Password:_____
Hint:_____
Notes:
_____
_____

Website:_____
Username:_____
Password:_____
Hint:_____
Notes:
_____
_____

Website:_____
Username:_____
Password:_____
Hint:_____
Notes:
_____
_____

Website:_____
Username:_____
Password:_____
Hint:_____
Notes:
_____
_____

Website:_____
Username:_____
Password:_____
Hint:_____
Notes:
_____
_____

Website:_____
Username:_____
Password:_____
Hint:_____
Notes:
_____
_____

Website:_____
Username:_____
Password:_____
Hint:_____
Notes:
_____
_____

Website:_____
Username:_____
Password:_____
Hint:_____
Notes:
_____
_____

Website:_____
Username:_____
Password:_____
Hint:_____
Notes:
_____
_____

Website:_____
Username:_____
Password:_____
Hint:_____
Notes:
_____
_____

Website:_____
Username:_____
Password:_____
Hint:_____
Notes:
_____
_____

Website:_____
Username:_____
Password:_____
Hint:_____
Notes:
_____
_____

Website:_____
Username:_____
Password:_____
Hint:_____
Notes:
_____
_____

Website:_____
Username:_____
Password:_____
Hint:_____
Notes:
_____
_____

Website:_____
Username:_____
Password:_____
Hint:_____
Notes:
_____
_____

Website:_____
Username:_____
Password:_____
Hint:_____
Notes:
_____
_____

Website:_____
Username:_____
Password:_____
Hint:_____
Notes:
_____
_____
_____

Website:_____
Username:_____
Password:_____
Hint:_____
Notes:
_____
_____
_____

Website:_____
Username:_____
Password:_____
Hint:_____
Notes:
_____
_____
_____

Website:_____
Username:_____
Password:_____
Hint:_____
Notes:
_____
_____
_____

Website:_____
Username:_____
Password:_____
Hint:_____
Notes:
_____
_____
_____

Website:_____
Username:_____
Password:_____
Hint:_____
Notes:
_____
_____
_____

Website:_____

Username:_____

Password:_____

Hint:_____

Notes:

_____

_____

Website:_____

Username:_____

Password:_____

Hint:_____

Notes:

_____

_____

Website:_____

Username:_____

Password:_____

Hint:_____

Notes:

_____

_____

Website:_____

Username:_____

Password:_____

Hint:_____

Notes:

_____

_____

Website:_____

Username:_____

Password:_____

Hint:_____

Notes:

_____

_____

Website:_____

Username:_____

Password:_____

Hint:_____

Notes:

_____

_____

Website:_____
Username:_____
Password:_____
Hint:_____
Notes:

_____
_____
_____

Website:_____
Username:_____
Password:_____
Hint:_____
Notes:

_____
_____
_____

Website:_____
Username:_____
Password:_____
Hint:_____
Notes:

_____
_____
_____

Website:_____
Username:_____
Password:_____
Hint:_____
Notes:

_____
_____
_____

Website:_____
Username:_____
Password:_____
Hint:_____
Notes:

_____
_____
_____

Website:_____
Username:_____
Password:_____
Hint:_____
Notes:

_____
_____
_____

Website:_____
Username:_____
Password:_____
Hint:_____
Notes:
_____
_____

Website:_____
Username:_____
Password:_____
Hint:_____
Notes:
_____
_____

Website:_____
Username:_____
Password:_____
Hint:_____
Notes:
_____
_____

Website:_____
Username:_____
Password:_____
Hint:_____
Notes:
_____
_____

Website:_____
Username:_____
Password:_____
Hint:_____
Notes:
_____
_____

Website:_____
Username:_____
Password:_____
Hint:_____
Notes:
_____
_____

Website:_____
Username:_____
Password:_____
Hint:_____
Notes:
_____
_____

Website:_____
Username:_____
Password:_____
Hint:_____
Notes:
_____
_____

Website:_____
Username:_____
Password:_____
Hint:_____
Notes:
_____
_____

Website:_____
Username:_____
Password:_____
Hint:_____
Notes:
_____
_____

Website:_____
Username:_____
Password:_____
Hint:_____
Notes:
_____
_____

Website:_____
Username:_____
Password:_____
Hint:_____
Notes:
_____
_____